Sefer Ha-Aggadah

· · · · · · ·

The Book of Legends
for Young Readers

§ ξ

ℰ ℰ

Adapted from *The Book of Legends:*

Sefer Ha-Aggadah, translated by William G. Braude

from the classic Hebrew work *Sefer Ha-Aggadah*,

edited by Hayim Nahman Bialik and

Yehoshua Hana Ravnitzky.

SEYMOUR ROSSEL

Sefer Ha-Aggadah

. . . .

The Book of Legends
for Young Readers

Volume 2 : TALES OF THE SAGES

Illustrated by JUDY DICK

UAHC Press · New York

For "Uncle" Eliot G. Spack—
I Samuel 20:42
S.R.

Library of Congress Cataloging-in-Publication Data
Rossel, Seymour.
Sefer ha-aggadah : the book of legends for young readers /
Seymour Rossel ; illustrated by Judy Dick.
        p.   cm.
"Adapted from The book of legends: Sefer ha-aggadah, translated by
William G. Braude from the classic Hebrew work Sefer ha-aggadah,
edited by Hayim Nahman Bialik and Yehoshua Hana Ravnitzky."
Includes bibliographical references.
ISBN 0-8074-0603-1 (alk. paper)
1. Bible stories, English—O.T. 2. Legends, Jewish. I. Dick, Judy, ill.
II. Sefer ha-aggadah.   III. Title.
BM107.R67   1996
296.1'9—DC20   96-8558
                                                                    CIP
                                                                    AC
                                                                    Rev.

This book is published by arrangement with Schocken Books, Inc.
This book is printed on acid-free paper.
Copyright © 1998 by Seymour Rossel
Manufactured in the United States of America
10 9 8 7 6 5 4 3 2 1

Contents

Introduction

Hayim Nahman Bialik was considered "the Hebrew national poet." His friend and partner Yehoshua Hana Ravnitzky was an editor, journalist, and publisher. When they decided to collect the legends and stories of the sages of talmudic times, they had a single purpose: to revive the Hebrew language. In the end, however, the book they created between 1908 and 1911 was more than just a way of enjoying the study of Hebrew. The six parts of *Sefer Ha-Aggadah*, "The Book of Legends," portrayed the entire world of Talmud, from its beginnings in the first century before the common era to the middle of the fifth century of the common era—a span of nearly five hundred years.

Aggadah means "legend," but Bialik and Ravnitzky knew that the word meant much more to the sages. Weaving stories around the Jewish heritage, the sages created a world filled with lessons and masterful teachings. These tales were shared at night by families in their homes. For the Jewish people through the ages, these stories were the magazines, books, radio, television, movies, and Internet. Stories were told and retold, traded, shaped, and embellished. Teachings were repeated in the name of the rabbis who had first taught them, and when the names of the rabbis had been forgotten, people just began the teachings with "Our sages taught..." or "Our rabbis said...." When people heard these words, they reacted the way we do today when someone begins, "Once upon a time ...."

The original *Sefer Ha-Aggadah* contains hundreds of stories, each one a gem, arranged into six parts. The first part is made up of legends about the Bible and its main characters and events. The second part contains stories of the sages themselves. The third part speaks of the people of Israel and their place in the world. The fourth part deals with legends about God and teachings about good and evil. The fifth part is a collection of legends about life in the Jewish community. And whatever would not fit into one of the other categories is found in part six—sayings; proverbs; teachings about nature; and even superstitions, witchcraft, and magical cures.

The first English-language translation of the entire *Sefer Ha-Aggadah* was completed by Rabbi William G. Braude in 1988 and published by Schocken Books in 1992. In 1993, the UAHC Press decided to create a version of this classic for young people. The first volume, published in 1996, contained legends of the Bible and biblical figures. This volume, "Tales of the Sages," is based on the second part of *Sefer Ha-Aggadah*.

Not all the legends told in *Sefer Ha-Aggadah* are appropriate for young readers. Some contain complex concepts requiring detailed explanations that would detract from the liveliness of the tales. Even the legends selected for this collection had to be "unpacked" from their compact form. Wherever possible, the author retained the narrative as it was found in the original. From time to time, however, tales were combined and parts were rearranged to achieve for young readers the clarity and colorful narration of Bialik and Ravnitzky's original. Recapturing the excitement of our ancestors when they heard and told these stories, this volume will bring us closer to the precious heritage passed on in writing and by word of mouth from generation to generation.

Welcome to the world of Jewish legend and lore. Welcome to a world created in ancient times, arranged in modern times, and set before you as a gateway between the past and the future. May these tales bring you closer to God and God's creation and set your steps firmly on the pathways of peace.

§1§

Honi the Circle Maker

No rain fell in the Land of Israel. The sun came by day and the moon by night, but no cloud darkened the skies. In the towns, the people worried. Without rain, there would be no water in the valleys. Without water, there would be no grain. Without grain, there would be no bread. If rain did not come soon, there would be hunger by the end of the year. Farmers would lose their farms. People in the cities might starve. All through the month of Adar, when rain should fall, people watched the skies for a sign of a cloud, but not even a wisp of white was seen.

Everyone came to the synagogue to pray for rain, but their prayers were not answered. The month of Adar passed, but the rain never came.

The elders of the town called a meeting to discuss their problem. "It may be that we have done something wrong," one of the elders said. "Perhaps God is angry with us."

"Could God have forgotten us?" asked another of the elders.

"In truth, we are not wise enough to know why God does not send the rain," said another. "And our prayers cannot force God to send it."

Everyone nodded. One of the elders continued: "We cannot force

God to help us. For most of the things we need, we can work or study. But when it comes to rain, only God can help."

Now the wisest elder stood and spoke: "Most of us are good people, but many of us hardly ever go to the synagogue. When we pray to God, we are like a dog or cat asking for food from its owner. God loves us, but it is as difficult for God to understand us as it is for us to understand our pets. Yet there is one among us who studies God's ways both night and day. He is a master of the Torah, a great teacher and sage. He is not like God's pet but more like a member of God's own family. Let us call on Honi to pray for us."

So the elders came to Honi, saying, "Pray for rain to fall. We must have rain or we shall suffer and die."

Honi prayed for rain. But no rain came.

"There must be a way to force God to bring the rain," Honi thought. He opened the Bible to find an answer. When he came to the books of the Prophets, he found the story of Habakkuk. "Here is the way," he said to the elders. "When Habakkuk wanted God to answer his questions, he stood inside a circle and waited. That is what I must do."

With the elders of the town following him, Honi climbed to the top of a hill. Using his walking stick, Honi drew a circle in the earth and stood inside the circle.

"Holy One, Ruler of the universe," Honi called out, "Your children have asked me to pray for rain. I swear that I shall not leave this circle until You have mercy on Your children and send them rain."

Honi stood in his circle and waited. From out of the east, a breeze blew and a single small gray cloud appeared like a dot. As it grew, Honi felt a few drops of rain fall on him. For a few minutes there was a gentle drizzle and then it stopped. The cloud passed over and the rain had passed.

The elders of the town said, "Truly, we have seen a miracle: God has answered your prayer. But this is not enough rain to make a difference to us, only enough to allow you to leave the circle."

Then Honi raised his voice to the heavens again. "Ruler of the universe, it is not for a drizzle that I prayed. I shall not leave this circle until You send a rain that will soak the land, fill the wells, and make the rivers rush."

This time there was no waiting. The skies darkened, the windows of the heavens opened wide, and rain gushed forth everywhere. Each and every drop could fill a bucket. The land was soaked in an instant. And still the rain beat against the earth.

Honi called out: "Holy One, I did not pray for such a rain. I only asked for a peaceful rain, a loving rain, a rain to save Your people."

At once, the rain turned gentle. It fell quietly from flowing white clouds, even as the sun shone through it. It watered the land and filled the wells. It flowed down the hillsides into the valley and filled the rivers. The elders called to Honi, "Look there!"

Honi looked where the elders pointed and saw that indeed the rivers were now flooding, and the wells were overflowing with water. The people were running for the tops of the hills to escape the rushing waters below. "If this continues," the elders said, "we shall all drown. As you prayed for rain to save our lives, now you must pray for it to end."

Honi turned his head to the heavens again. "Holy One, we thank You for the miracle You have done for us. Now hear the cries of Your people: When You ignore them, they seek Your voice. When You are angry with them, they cannot stand Your anger. When You give them too much of a good thing, they cannot bear Your goodness. Be gentle with them. Let the rain end so You may hear their words of thanks."

The breeze came again from the east. The clouds blew away; the

skies cleared; and the rain stopped falling. Honi left his circle and returned home. The people went to gather the mushrooms that sprouted after the rain.

The next day, Simeon ben Shetah sent word to Honi: "You have acted like a spoiled brat. You are like a child who says to his parents, 'I want a hot bath.' So they heat water and bathe him. Then the child says, 'I want a cold bath.' So they bring cold water and bathe him. Then the child says, 'I want grapes and dates, walnuts and almonds, peaches and pomegranates to eat.' So they bring him fruits and nuts. This time God has listened to you as parents listen to a spoiled child. But, beware, parents soon run out of patience. If you try to force God to work a miracle for you again, you may not be so lucky."

Honi never again tried to force God to answer a prayer. Yet the people remembered what Honi had done for them, and from that time forth, they called him Honi the Circle Maker. (2,I:6)

From the Aggadah
BUYING A DONKEY

Rabbi Simeon ben Shetah went to the marketplace to buy a donkey. When he saw one he liked, he asked the Arab for the price and paid for it. Then he led the donkey home. His students came for their lesson, and they saw the new donkey. "It looks like a fine animal," they said. And they went to look at it closely.

Suddenly, they came running to Simeon's house. "Master," they said to him, "look what we found tied around the donkey's neck." They showed Simeon a little bag on a string. When they opened the bag, they found a beautiful jewel inside. "You thought you were buying just a donkey," they said. "But you have bought a jewel worth

ten times the price of the donkey. Surely, God has given you a gift as a reward for all your learning."

Simeon said, "I bought only the donkey. I did not buy the jewel."

"But master," the students said, "if you buy a field and a treasure is buried in the field, then the treasure belongs to you. So, too, if you buy a donkey and a jewel happens to be tied around the donkey's neck, the jewel belongs to you. That is the law."

"You are correct," said Simeon. "That is the law. But when it comes to helping others, the law is only the least we can do. We have to learn how to go beyond the law to bring peace to the world."

So Simeon returned the jewel to the Arab in the marketplace. From that time on, the Arab was heard to say, "Blessed be the God of Simeon ben Shetah." (2,I:4)

BUYING TORAH

Hillel and Shebna were brothers. Shebna became a merchant, and he made a lot of money. But Hillel studied Torah and hardly ever had a coin to spare. All the same, it was Hillel who became famous throughout Israel. Students came from near and far to listen to him teach.

One day, Shebna came to Hillel and said, "Why should I be rich, and you be poor? Let's be partners. We can share the profits."

Hillel shook his head. In his heart, he knew the answer that heaven would give to Shebna. "You cannot buy Torah," he told his brother. "You could give me all your wealth and profit, and still I could not share with you a word of Torah. The only way for you to share in the world of Torah is to study it yourself." (2,I:11)

§2§

The Sleeping Sage

Rabbi Yohanan was reading the Book of Psalms with his students when they came to the verse that said: "When the Holy One brought back those who returned to Zion, we were like those who dream." Yohanan told his students: "When the First Temple was destroyed, the people were taken to Babylonia. Seventy years passed like a dream. Then God brought us back to the Land of Israel."

Then one student asked, "Can a person really dream for seventy years?"

Yohanan laughed. "Not just any person. But once there was a very holy man named Honi who asked the very same question you are asking. The sages say that God answered his question. So let me tell you his story."

And this is the story that Yohanan told:

§ It was a lovely day and Honi went out walking. He crossed a small stream, and on the other side, he saw an old man planting a carob tree. Honi was puzzled. He scratched his beard and asked, "Old man, don't you know that it takes seventy years for a carob tree to bear fruit?"

The old man said, "I am old, but I am not a fool. Of course, I know that it will take seventy years for this tree to grow and bear fruit."

"But you are old," Honi said. "Why not plant a peach tree or a date palm? You might live long enough to eat the fruit of those trees. Why should you plant a carob tree, knowing that you will not live long enough to eat its fruit?"

The old man replied, "When I came into this world, I found fully grown carob trees waiting for me. So I am planting this carob tree for my children."

Honi left the old man and continued walking. Suddenly, he felt very tired. He sat down beneath a shade tree to rest and fell fast asleep. As he slept, plants grew up around him, hiding him from sight. Farmers came and plowed the nearby fields, but they never saw him. Shepherds led their flocks nearby, but they did not see him. Time passed, and the trees grew thick around him. His beard reached his belly and still went on growing. Seventy years passed while Honi slept and dreamed.

One day, the breeze blew through the branches of the trees, and a leaf tickled Honi's cheek. He stretched his arms and rubbed the sleep from his eyes. "I must have dozed off," Honi thought. Looking down, he saw that his beard ended at his knees. "I have been sleeping a long time," Honi thought. Looking around, he saw trees on every side of him. "I must have slept a very long time," Honi thought.

He made a path through the trees and walked back toward the stream. Then he saw a man gathering carobs from a tree. "This is the same tree I watched the old man plant," Honi thought. He spoke to the man. "Are you the man who planted this tree?"

The man smiled. "Old man," he said to Honi, "don't you know it takes seventy years for a carob tree to bear fruit? I am gathering carob from a tree my grandfather planted."

"Can it be?" Honi wondered. "Have I truly slept for seventy years?"

He went home, but the town had changed, and his house was gone. He asked a woman, "Do you know the son of Honi the Circle Maker?" She answered, "Honi's son is no longer in this world, but his grandson is."

Then Honi said: "I am Honi the Circle Maker."

The old woman laughed. "If you are Honi," she said, "then I am Queen Esther, and today is Purim."

Honi went through the whole town. To everyone he met, he announced, "I am Honi the Circle Maker." But no one believed him.

Looking for a place to sit, he found the house of study and entered it. There he heard the teachers telling the pupils, "In the old days, when there was a hard lesson to learn, our fathers would ask Honi the Circle Maker to explain it." Then Honi called out, "But I am Honi!" The students laughed, and the teachers shook their heads. No one would believe him.

So Honi crossed the stream once more and sat down beneath the carob tree. He recalled the old man's words: "When I came into this world, I found fully grown carob trees waiting for me. So I am planting this carob tree for my children." Suddenly, these words seemed very wise. Honi thought, "When I came into this world, I found wisdom waiting for me. Still, I studied and taught so there would be wisdom for my children. Each of us has only one lifetime in this world, but together with our children and grandchildren we can share many lives."

Then Honi turned his face to the heavens and spoke to God: "I have learned the meaning of my life. Now my time is passed, and the time of my grandchildren has come." And Honi smiled and fell asleep forever. (2,I:7)

From the Aggadah
HILLEL'S WIFE

An important man came to dinner at Hillel's home. All that day, Hillel's wife had worked to make a perfect meal for their guest. But before they sat down to eat, a poor man appeared at the door. Hillel's wife greeted him and said, "Hillel is busy with a guest. How may I help you?"

"Mine is both a glad and sad story," the man answered. "Today is the day of my wedding. And for that reason I am glad. But I have no food to feed my wedding guests, and I have no money for food. And for that reason I am sad. I have come to ask Hillel for a loan to buy food."

Then Hillel's wife said, "We have something better than money to give you," and she took the meal she had made and gave it to the poor man. But as soon as the man had left with his wedding feast, she heard her husband calling, "My dear, is dinner almost ready?"

She called back to him: "It will be a few minutes, my dear."

She set about baking bread, cooking a pot of stew, and fixing a salad. An hour passed and then another. At last, she called her husband and his guest to the table, placing the meal before them.

"My dear," asked Hillel, "why did you not serve us sooner?"

At once, Hillel's wife told the whole story: how the poor man had come to the door and how she had given him the meal that she had worked all day to prepare so he could serve it at his wedding.

Then Hillel smiled. "My dear," he said, "I asked only because I knew you had a good reason for waiting." He turned to his guest, saying, "You see, everything my wife does, she does for the sake of heaven." (2,I:18)

COMFORT FOR YOHANAN

The son of Rabban Yohanan ben Zakkai died, and Rabban Yohanan's students came to comfort him.

One student began, "Remember Adam and Eve! They had a son who died, but they were comforted by having another son."

Rabban Yohanan said, "I am still grieving over my own son. Do you have to remind me of the grief of Adam and Eve?"

A second student began, "Remember Job! He lost all his sons and daughters, and God gave him a new family."

Rabban Yohanan said, "I am saddened by the loss of one son. Do you have to remind me of the many losses Job suffered?"

A third began, "Remember David! He lost a son and was comforted when God sent him Solomon, whose name means 'peace.'"

Rabban Yohanan said, "I am not at peace over the loss of my son. Should I also have to suffer because David lost a son?"

Then Rabbi Eleazar ben Arakh spoke: "A king once came and gave a gem to a man, saying, 'Guard this for me.' Every day, the man would see the gem and worry: 'When will the king come to take back this gem from me so it will be safe?' You had a son. He studied the Torah, and he studied the laws and legends of our people. In the end, God asked for the return of your precious gem, and you returned him safely. You have done all you could do for the sake of heaven."

Rabban Yohanan said, "Eleazar, your words are wise. You have made me feel better. This is the way people should be comforted." (2,I:51)

❧ 3 ❧

Hillel on the Roof

Shemayah and Avtalyon were among the greatest teachers of Torah in Jerusalem. Far away in Babylonia, Hillel heard of them and decided to study with them. Being poor, he made the long journey to Jerusalem on foot. After many days of walking, he came to the gate of the house of study and said to the watchman, "I have come to study with the sages." But the watchman said, "To study, you must pay. To come into the house of study, you must give me half a *tropaic*."

So Hillel went to work. He earned one *tropaic* every day. Half of it, he used for food and a place to stay. The other half, he gave to the watchman at the house of study. And, truth be known, Hillel was always more hungry for the words of Torah and the teachings of Shemayah and Avtalyon than he was for food to eat.

One Friday, Hillel could find no work at all. He had no money to pay the watchman, and this made him very sad. He felt as gray as the cloud-filled sky. Indeed, without the words of his teachers to warm him, he was nearly as cold as the winter day.

"I have no money today," he told the watchman. But the watchman had no pity on him. "No money, no lesson," the man said.

Then Hillel had an idea. He climbed to the roof of the house of study and stretched himself out on it so he would not fall. And he put his head over the skylight, covering half the opening in the roof. In this way, he could listen to Shemayah and Avtalyon.

Hillel did not notice the snow beginning to fall. He was listening to the lesson.

§ ê

Morning came. It was the Sabbath. Shemayah and Avtalyon rose, wrapped themselves in warm clothing, and entered the house of study.

"It is a cold day, Brother Shemayah," said Avtalyon, crossing his arms and shivering. "But because it is Shabbat, we are not permitted to make a fire to warm us."

"Yes, a cold day, Brother Avtalyon," Shemayah agreed. "But tell me, do you not notice a strange thing?"

"What is that?"

"Every day, this house of study is bright with light, but today it seems dark. Tell me, is the day cloudy?" asked Shemayah.

"It was clear from my window," said Avtalyon.

Then they both looked up at the skylight. There they saw the shape of a young man like a dark shadow beneath the snow.

"I see a shape like a frozen person, Brother Shemayah," Avtalyon said.

"I see it, too, Brother Avtalyon," Shemayah answered.

They ran out of the house of study and climbed to the roof. There was Hillel covered over by the snow.

"Quickly," Avtalyon said, "let us save the young man if we can."

So they called the watchman to help them, and together all three carried the frozen Hillel from the roof into the house of study. They took the snow from his body and bathed him with warm water.

While they were doing so, the watchman said: "It is my fault, masters. The boy had no money, and I told him he could not enter unless he paid. He must have climbed to the roof to listen through the skylight."

"No," said Shemayah kindly, "it is our fault and not yours. For we instructed you, 'Do not let students enter without paying,' and you were doing only what we asked."

"That is true," said Avtalyon, "but from now on, you are to let this student in for the lesson even if he has no money at all."

They were rubbing him with warm towels, but Hillel was still shivering wildly.

"We must build a fire to warm him, Brother Shemayah," said Avtalyon. And Shemayah fetched logs for the fire.

"But it is the Sabbath, and we are forbidden to build a fire on the Sabbath," said the watchman.

"I am the teacher," said Avtalyon. "Learn this, my friend: To save a life, we are permitted to break the law, even the Sabbath law."

"Truly, said Shemayah as he lit the fire, "this man deserves to have the Sabbath broken on his behalf."

"Yes," said Avtalyon as he sat the boy by the open fire. "His love of learning is great. It is certain that one day this Hillel will become a great sage in Israel." (2,I:12)

From the Aggadah

ONE GOLDEN LEG

Hanina was a kind man. He loved his wife very much. If only he were a rich man, he would get a servant to carry the water for her. He would get another servant to make the bread and cook the meals for her. He sighed. If only he were a rich man!

Hanina's wife once said to him, "You work hard, and I work hard. Yet we have very little. How long shall we suffer?"

"What shall we do?" he asked.

"I have heard that the reward for studying Torah in this life is riches and joy in the world-to-come. Why not pray for God to send you some of the riches that you will have in the world-to-come?"

Hanina prayed until he could pray no more. He felt dizzy and sat down. His head was still reeling when he thought he saw a hand reaching down from heaven to give him a long stick of gold. "Heaven has heard my prayer," he said to himself, "and God has given me gold from the world-to-come."

Before he could tell his wife the good news, Hanina fell asleep and dreamed. In his dream, he and his wife were in the world-to-come. All the sages were sitting with their families at tables of gold. And each table had three golden legs. But he and his wife were sitting at a table that had only two legs so they had to hold up the table with their hands.

"Are you happy with this table of two legs?" Hanina asked his wife.

"What happened to the other leg?" she inquired.

"I prayed for heaven to send us riches from the world-to-come, and I was given one of the three golden legs from our table."

Hanina's wife shook her head. "When you wake up from this dream," she said, "you must pray for heaven to take back the leg of gold."

Hanina awoke from his dream and prayed that the leg of gold be taken back. He opened his eyes and looked at his hand. His hand was open, too, and the leg of gold was gone. Then he looked at his wife. "My dear, I have prayed twice to heaven, once for heaven to give us riches and once for heaven to take the riches back. In truth, we are already rich. In this world, our love is more gold than we will ever need." (2,I:57)

THE UGLY SAGE

A beautiful princess saw Rabbi Joshua in the marketplace. "What a pity you are so ugly," she said. "You have so much wisdom, but your God put it into such an ugly body."

"Does your father have much wine?" Rabbi Joshua asked the princess. She nodded, "Very much."

"In what does he keep his wine?" She answered, "In clay jugs."

"Clay jugs are very well for the common people," said Rabbi Joshua, "but you are royal folk."

Then the princess asked, "In what should we keep our wine?"

"You are so important," Rabbi Joshua replied, "that you should keep your wine in jugs of silver and gold."

The princess went off and told her father what the rabbi had said.

Then the emperor placed all his wine in jugs of silver and gold. The wine touched the metal and began to sour. Before long, all the wine had become vinegar.

The emperor asked his daughter, "Who gave you this advice?"

"The wise Rabbi Joshua."

So the emperor called for Rabbi Joshua and asked him, "Why did you tell my daughter to place wine in silver and gold?"

"She thought all things of beauty should come in beautiful containers," answered Rabbi Joshua. "I was just teaching her a lesson: We should not look at the outside to tell if something is ugly or beautiful—all depends on what is inside." (2,I:106)

§4§

Two Torahs

There were two great teachers of Torah in Jerusalem. One was Hillel, and the other was Shammai. Both formed schools for their students, and both had many students. Both were very busy. Yet it was said that Hillel was always ready to take time to help anyone. So our sages loved to tell stories about Hillel's kindness and wisdom.

Once a non-Jew came to Shammai and asked, "How many Torahs do the Jews believe in?"

Shammai answered, "Jews believe in two Torahs: the Written Torah that is in the Five Books of Moses and the Spoken Torah that explains the Written Torah."

The non-Jew said, "I can trust what is written down, but how do I know I can trust what is spoken? I will become your student if you promise to teach me only your Written Torah."

This made Shammai angry. "How can you be my student if you will not trust what I speak?" he asked. "Be gone. And do not return to my school."

The same fellow came to see Hillel and asked the same question, "How many Torahs do the Jews believe in?" And Hillel answered in the same way. Then the non-Jew said, "I will become your student if you promise to teach me only your Written Torah." And Hillel agreed.

On the first day, Hillel taught the non-Jew the Hebrew alphabet from its beginning: *"alef, bet, gimel, dalet,"* and so on. But on the second day, Hillel taught the alphabet backwards: *"tav, shin, reish, kof,"* and so on.

The non-Jew said, "Wait a minute! Yesterday, you taught me that the alphabet begins with *alef*, and today you say it begins with *tav*. Which is correct?"

"Now you see," replied Hillel, "that you must trust me even when it comes to what is written. So you must also learn to trust me when it comes to the Spoken Torah."

In this way, Hillel gained a student.

Another time, a non-Jew came to Shammai and said, "I wish to study with you if you can teach me the whole Torah, all of it, while I stand on one foot."

Shammai took a ruler from his desk and shook it at the fellow. "Be gone," he yelled out. "And do not return to my school with anymore of your silliness."

The same fellow came to see Hillel and made the same request, "Teach me the whole Torah while I stand on one foot."

Hillel replied, "What is hateful to you, do not do to another. This is the whole Torah, all of it. Now, go and study it."

In this way, Hillel gained another student.

It happened again. This time, a non-Jew came to Shammai and said, "I wish to study with you if you will make me the High Priest of your Temple." Shammai picked up his ruler and chased the man away.

This time, Hillel smiled. "Come and study with me," he offered. "But first, answer a question for me."

The non-Jew asked, "What question shall I answer?"

Hillel said, "Would you like to live in a country where the king did not know the laws of the country?"

The fellow shook his head. "A king should know the laws so he can be fair."

"That is a good answer," said Hillel. "If you wish to become the High Priest of the Temple, you must first learn the laws of the Temple."

The fellow nodded. "That makes sense," he agreed.

Then Hillel taught the non-Jew the laws of the Temple, adding, "And the High Priest can come only from one born to the family of Aaron."

"Then I could never be the High Priest!" said the non-Jew.

"Not the High Priest," answered Hillel, "but see what a wonderful student of Torah you are! You understand the laws even as I teach them."

Then the fellow smiled at Hillel, saying, "O gentle Hillel, may you be blessed! I came to you to gain glory for myself, but you have taught me the spirit of Jewish study."

In this way, Hillel gained another student.

There came a time, the sages said, when these three fellows met on their way to Hillel's house of study. Each of them told his story—how he put his request to Shammai and then to Hillel. And all three said, "If we had listened to Shammai, we would never have become converts, but Hillel's gentleness turned us to the ways of Torah." (2,I:15)

From the Aggadah
WISE CHILDREN

The students of Rabbi Joshua asked him, "Why do you always pay such close attention to everything we say?"

Rabbi Joshua answered, "I am your teacher, but that does not

mean I always know more than you. I listen carefully because I have been taught many good lessons even by little children."

"What have you learned from children?" they asked.

Rabbi Joshua told two stories:

§ I was walking between two towns, and I saw a road that cut through a field. I thought, "My way will be shorter if I take that road." So I started to walk through the field. But when I had walked only a short way, a little girl called out to me.

"Master," she began, "are you so cruel that you would trample the grain in this field?"

"No," I replied, "but this is surely a path that many feet have traveled before mine. The grain here is already trampled."

"That is true," said the little girl. "It was trampled by others as cruel as you. They, too, set their feet to go through the field instead of around it."

"You are absolutely correct," I told the girl. Then I turned back and went around the field.

§ I was walking between two towns when I saw a little boy sitting by a crossroads. I asked him, "My son, by which of these roads should I go to the town?"

First, he pointed to one road, saying, "This one is the shorter road but longer." Then he pointed at the other road, saying, "This road is the longer road but shorter."

Being very tired, I decided to take the shorter road, but after I walked some distance, I found that the road came to an end. Bushes and weeds blocked the way to the town. So I turned back and returned to the crossroads. The little boy was still there.

"My son," I inquired, "did you not tell me that the road I took was shorter?"

"You listened, but you did not hear," said the little boy. "I said that the road you took was shorter but longer. It is longer because you would have to struggle through the weeds and thorns to get to town. But the other road, O master, is longer but shorter. It ends in the center of the town."

So I kissed the boy on the head and said to him, "We are truly blessed, for even the youngest children of Israel are wise." (2,I:114)

THE EMPEROR AND THE SUN

Rabbi Joshua was visiting with the emperor, when the emperor asked, "Tell me, wise sage, does the world have a ruler?"

Rabbi Joshua answered, "God is the Ruler of the world."

"And who created heaven and earth?" the emperor asked.

Rabbi Joshua answered, "In the Torah it is written, 'In the beginning God created heaven and earth.'"

Then the emperor asked, "Why is God not like the emperor of Rome? God should be seen twice a year so that people may know God and worship the Ruler of the world."

"The Torah tells us that God is too powerful for people to see. God has said, 'No person shall see Me and live.'"

"Nevertheless, if you do not show God to me," the emperor demanded, "I will not believe there truly is a God."

Rabbi Joshua took the emperor out into the garden. It was noon, and the sun was high in the sky. Rabbi Joshua said, "Now look into the sun, and you will see God."

The emperor tried to look into the sun, but as he did, he was forced to cover his eyes to keep them from burning. "I cannot look into the sun," he said.

"Listen to yourself," said Rabbi Joshua. "If you cannot look into the sun, which is just one of God's creations, then how can you expect to look at God?" (2,I:116)

§ 5 §

Torah Is Not in Heaven

Our sages taught: In the Torah, God gave us all the laws we need. Since the time of the Torah, people have to settle arguments between themselves.

The students asked: "How do we know this?"

The sages answered: "From the story of Rabbi Eliezer and the oven of Akhnai."

§ In the time of Rabbi Eliezer, a new kind of oven was invented. Old ovens were made of bricks or clay. The new oven was made like a layer cake, with coils of clay separated by layers of sand. The whole oven was then covered over by cement. It was called the Akhnai oven. Some say that it was called this because the name of the inventor was Akhnai. Some say that it was called Akhnai because *Akhnai* means "snake," and the clay seemed coiled like a snake ready to strike. But some say it was called Akhnai because the rabbis encircled it with many arguments as if a snake had wrapped itself around the oven.

The problem was, would the oven be *kosher* if it were used for meat and a drop of milk fell on it? If it were no longer *kosher*, then it would have to be replaced. But if it were still *kosher*, then it could still be used. Rabbi Eliezer argued that the oven would always be *kosher*. It could not be spoiled because it was not made of one piece and so it was not one thing. The rest of the rabbis argued that the cement that covered the oven made it all one piece and so it would no longer be *kosher* if any part of it was spoiled. Rabbi Eliezer argued fiercely, but the rabbis would not agree with him.

The rabbis were sitting on the benches near the walls of the house of study in Lydda. A small stream ran nearby. And the trees shaded the rabbis from the sun. It was a beautiful day, but Rabbi Eliezer paid no attention to the sunshine and the breeze. He argued and argued until it was clear that he could not win.

Then he turned to all the other rabbis and said, "I will prove to you that I am right and you are wrong. If I am right, let this carob tree move."

As sudden as a flash of lightning, the carob tree jumped from the ground and flew across the stream. And just as suddenly, it planted itself on the other bank of the stream. The rabbis were amazed. They could hardly believe their eyes. For a moment, they sat quietly, lost in thought.

At last, one rabbi stood and said, "Carob trees do not know the law. You can't prove that you are right by asking a carob tree to move."

Rabbi Eliezer would not give up. "If I am right," he said, "let the stream flow backward."

As the rabbis watched, the water in the stream came to a complete stop. Then the water began to run uphill toward the mountains of Judea.

A rabbi stood and said, "Streams do not know the law. You can't prove you are right by asking a stream to flow backward."

Rabbi Eliezer refused to give up. "If I am right," he said, "let the walls of the house of study fall."

The brick walls of the house of study began to tremble. The rabbis jumped from their seats and started to run for safety.

"Wait," cried Rabbi Joshua, pointing to the walls. "You walls have no right to make laws for Israel! You must stand and not fall."

Listening to Rabbi Joshua, the walls refused to fall. But because Rabbi Eliezer had asked them to fall, the walls leaned a little. And from that day on, the walls of the house of study at Lydda always leaned over the rabbis when they sat outdoors on their benches.

When they saw that it was safe, the rabbis took their seats again. One of them asked, "Rabbi Eliezer, why not give up and admit that you are beaten?"

Rabbi Eliezer crossed his arms and spoke again. "I can prove that I am correct." Then he raised his voice and cried out, "If I am right, let heaven say so."

In a deep and rolling thunder, an echo came from the distant hills and filled the heavens with sound. "Rabbi Eliezer knows the law. Why do you argue with him?"

Now Rabbi Joshua stood again. "God has told us in the Torah, 'Torah is not in heaven.' We Jews pay no attention to voices from the sky because long ago the Torah told us, 'The majority rules.' When we rabbis argue about a law, we take a vote to see who wins."

Then the rabbis voted. Rabbi Eliezer cast one vote for his argument. All the other rabbis voted against him. Rabbi Eliezer lost the argument. Thus the rabbis taught us that we must not rely on trees or streams or walls or even heaven itself to settle our arguments; we must settle them ourselves. (2,I:98)

From the Aggadah
LET ME BUY YOU A TOWN

Although Rabbi Tarfon was very rich, he did not often give money to the poor. One time, he was walking through the streets of the town with Rabbi Akiva. Akiva asked, "Tarfon, how would you like me to buy one or two towns for you?"

Rabbi Tarfon said, "Yes, towns would be good to own." He gave four thousand gold *dinar*s to Rabbi Akiva.

What did Rabbi Akiva do? He took the money and divided it among the poor students in the house of study.

A little later, Rabbi Tarfon met Rabbi Akiva in the market. "Where are the towns that you bought for me?" he asked.

"Come, I will show you," answered Akiva. He took Rabbi Tarfon by the hand and led him to the house of study. There he found one of the poor students reading from the Book of Psalms. He pointed to a verse and told the child to read it aloud.

The child read, "He has divided it among the people; he has given to those in need; he will always be called righteous."

Then Rabbi Akiva spoke to Rabbi Tarfon, saying, "This is the town I bought for you."

Rabbi Tarfon hugged Rabbi Akiva and kissed him on the forehead. "You are my teacher and my friend," he said. "With your wisdom, you teach me. By what you do, you prove that you are my friend."

Rabbi Tarfon took more golden *dinar*s from his purse and pressed them into Akiva's hands. He smiled and said, "Now, go and buy me another town." (2,I:132)

THE BLIND MAN AND THE LANTERN

Rabbi Yose used to tell this story: He was walking along a path through a forest. It was night, and there was no moon to brighten the skies. Through the trees, he could see tiny pinpoints of light, the scattered stars. In his hand, he held a lantern to light the road ahead. From time to time, he passed other people walking. And most of them held a lantern, too. This made him think. From above, the earth would look much like the sky: The ground would be as black as the heaven at night, and each lantern would be a pinpoint of light, an earthly star.

Just then he approached a traveler different from all the others. From the way the man held his head—high, with his eyes facing directly before him—and from the way he walked—testing the ground with a stick in one hand—Rabbi Yose knew that the man was blind. So he was surprised to see that this man also carried a lit lantern.

"*Shalom aleichem*," he called out to the man, "peace be with you."

"*Aleichem shalom*, peace be with you, too," the man replied.

"Tell me, sir," said Yose. "Is it true that you are blind and cannot see?"

"It is true."

"Tell me, kind sir," said Yose. "Is it true that you cannot see during the day and you cannot see at night?"

"It is true."

"So it makes no difference to you whether it is day or night?" asked Yose.

"No difference," the man answered.

"Then, tell me, kind sir, why do you need to carry a lantern?"

The blind man smiled. "You ask questions like a teacher," he said. "Are you a teacher?"

"I am," replied Rabbi Yose.

"With all your wisdom, can you not guess why a blind man should carry a lantern at night?"

"I cannot," Rabbi Yose answered. "Pray, tell me."

"As long as I have my lantern, people can see me and see the road, too. So they can save me from vines, thorns, and holes. If I did not carry my lantern at night, and if you did not carry your lantern, then both of us would be blind." (2,I:240)

❧ 6 ❧

"This Too Is for Good"

There was a certain man called Nahum of Gamzo. Why was he called Gamzo? Because whenever something went wrong for him, he would always say, "*Gam zo letovah*, 'This too is for good.'" And things were always going wrong for him. He was blind in both eyes. He said, "*Gam zo letovah*, 'This too is for good.' Now I can learn to look into my heart to love God more." He was crippled in both legs. He said, "*Gam zo letovah*, 'This too is for good.' Now I can spend more time in studying Torah and less time walking from place to place." His body was covered with sores. "*Gam zo letovah*, 'This too is for good.' Now I can stop thinking about being handsome and pay closer attention to the beauty of what God has created." His house fell down, leaving only ruins. He said, "*Gam zo letovah*, 'This too is for good.' Now I can spend less time making my home a better place and spend more time making God's world a better place." No matter what happened to him, no matter how bad it seemed to others, Nahum of Gamzo would merely say, "*Gam zo letovah*, 'This too is for good.'"

One time, the Jews decided to send a gift to the emperor. They came to Nahum. "We wish you to take a chest full of diamonds and pearls to the emperor."

Nahum said, "Why should I be chosen for such a great honor?"

"Because no matter what, you always find a way to make things good," they said.

So Nahum loaded the chest of jewels on one donkey, climbed on another donkey, and set out to see the emperor. On the way, he stopped for the night at an inn. "I am on my way to see the emperor," he said to the innkeeper, "and I need a room for the night." Then the innkeeper helped Nahum put the chest in his room.

"This chest is very heavy," said the innkeeper to Nahum. "It must be filled with books."

"Not books," said Nahum, "it is filled with precious gems."

The innkeeper smiled. When Nahum was fast asleep, the innkeeper crept into his room and stole all the diamonds and pearls from the chest. Then he filled the chest with earth. The next morning, he helped Nahum load the chest back on the donkey. "You must be very careful with this treasure," he told Nahum. "You should not tell everyone what is in this chest. Someone might try to steal it from you."

Nahum thanked the innkeeper and went on his way. When he got to the emperor's palace, the guards brought Nahum and the chest to the emperor. "I have brought a gift from your loyal friends, the Jews of Israel," said Nahum.

Then the chest was opened. The emperor was very angry at what he saw. "Is this the kind of gift that the Jews send to me? A chest full of dirt? Am I not the emperor of Rome? Do I not deserve gifts of gold and silver, gifts of precious spices, gifts of jewels and silks?" Then the emperor said, "I will show you what I think of your gift. I will have you tortured and killed."

Nahum said, "*Gam zo letovah*, 'This too is for good.'"

"How can this be good?" demanded the emperor. But just at that moment, the king's wise man whispered in the king's ear, "This must

be special dirt. For I once heard how Abraham, the father of the Jews, threw earth at his enemies, and the earth turned into swords and arrows and drove his enemies away."

"We shall see," said the emperor. He sent the chest of earth to where his soldiers were fighting. In the heat of the battle, the emperor's soldiers threw the dirt in their enemies' eyes. And when the dirt blinded their enemies, the soldiers defeated them. Then they sent word back to the emperor, saying, "Your secret weapon has helped us to conquer a city!"

The emperor called for Nahum Gamzo. "Your God has worked a miracle for me. Now, I will show you honor." He called his soldiers to bring a chest larger than the one the Jews had sent and to fill it with diamonds and pearls. The emperor announced, "I give these gems and pearls as a gift to the Jews." And he sent Nahum on his way.

Nahum stopped at the same inn for the night, and once again the innkeeper helped him with his chest. "This chest is bigger and heavier than before," said the innkeeper. "You must have bought even more books."

But Nahum answered, "No. I gave the emperor what was in the chest, and the emperor gave me a gift of diamonds and pearls."

The next morning, after Nahum left, the innkeeper filled a heavy chest with earth and took it to the emperor. "Great Caesar of Rome," the innkeeper said, "I have brought you a great gift, the same earth that was given to you by Nahum of Gamzo."

"We shall see," the emperor replied. He sent the earth to his soldiers. But this time, when the soldiers threw the dirt at their enemies, their enemies were wise to the trick and covered their eyes with their hands. Then they drove back the emperor's soldiers, defeating them. When the emperor heard how his soldiers had lost the battle, he had the innkeeper put to death.

That day, Nahum brought the emperor's chest to the Jews. "You have truly worked a miracle," they told him. "We sent you with a small treasure, and you returned to us an even greater treasure."

All Nahum said was, *"Gam zo letovah, 'This too is for good.'"* (2,I:126 and 127)

From the Aggadah
MOSES AND AKIVA

Rabbi Judah remembered a story that he heard from that great sage Rav: When Moses arrived in heaven, he saw God decorating some of the letters of the Torah with little crowns. Moses asked, "Why are You decorating these letters? Why not just write down what You want to say so it will be easy for everyone to understand it?"

God said, "After many generations, a great teacher will come to Israel, and his name will be Akiva ben Joseph. He will see these crowns and understand their meaning, and he will teach the Jews many wondrous things about each and every little crown."

"Ruler of the universe," Moses said, "allow me to see teacher."

God replied, "Turn around." When Moses turned aroun in the back of the house of study, where Akiva was teaching _.__ __ the students listened and smiled at the lessons Akiva taught, but Moses could not understand the lessons at all. Moses' heart was heavy with sadness.

Then one of the students asked Akiva, "Master, where did you learn these lessons?"

Akiva answered, "These were the laws given by God to Moses at Mount Sinai."

Moses felt better at that. Turning around again, he said to God, "O Holy One, You have such a great teacher as this Akiva, why did You choose to give the Torah through me and not through him?"

God replied, "You were the right teacher for your generation, and he is the right teacher for his generation." (2,I:140)

THE GLOW OF THE SAGES

A Roman princess saw Rabbi Judah bar Ilai and noticed that his face was glowing. She said, "Old man, you must have eaten so many pigs that their oil shows on your skin."

"I have not eaten any pigs," said Rabbi Judah.

"Then you must be so happy because you are a money lender who has made a vast fortune," she said.

"I am not a money lender," responded Rabbi Judah.

"Then you must be all aglow because you have drunk too much wine," she said.

"I drink wine on the Sabbath, when it is required," said Rabbi

Judah, "and the four cups of wine that I must drink at Passover always make me feel weak for weeks."

The princess asked, "Then why does your face shine with that special glow?"

Rabbi Judah answered, "This is the glow of the teachers of Torah. As the wise Solomon used to say, 'It is wisdom that brightens the face.'" (2,I:259)

§7§

Rachel

Rachel was the daughter of a rich man named Kalba Savua. She lived in a beautiful room. The floor was a mosaic of birds and lions made of Roman tiles. The window looked out on a garden of roses. Her father and mother loved her. They gave her everything she wanted. Everything, except for one thing. Rachel was lonely. She was old enough to marry, but she knew none of the young men in town. "When it is time for you to marry," Kalba Savua often said, "I will find the right man for you."

One morning, Kalba Savua called for Rachel. "I need some help, my dear. Get water from the barrel and take it to the shepherds who watch my flocks."

Kalba Savua had many flocks, and Rachel had to carry the water from one flock to another. At each stop, the shepherd boys smiled at her. She studied each of them closely, thinking, "This one is too old for me," "This one is too silly for me," or "This one is too tall for me." The afternoon was slipping away by the time she reached the last flock.

The last shepherd boy was not very handsome. He was too shy to look at her. But she studied him. He was dressed in an old robe, a sign that he came from a poor family. His hair was not brushed or oiled.

Yet, something about him made her want to stop awhile.

She started playfully, asking, "Will you always be a shepherd?"

He shook his head. He was even too shy to speak! "What else can you do?" she pressed. "Can you forge iron or make sandals?"

He shook his head. "I would like to read," he said softly.

"You cannot read or write?" she asked.

He shook his head again.

Rachel went home. But her thoughts kept turning to the simple shepherd. He was poor but that did not bother her. She felt special when she was near him, and she liked him ever so much for being shy. Of course, her father would never let her marry a common shepherd.

A few days passed, and Rachel went to visit her shepherd. As she came closer, she knew for certain that she loved him. "Be brave," she told herself. "He is too shy to tell me what is in his heart. I will have to talk for both of us."

They sat awhile, watching the sheep. Then Rachel asked, "What is your name?"

"I am Akiva ben Joseph," the young man said.

"Akiva," she repeated, liking the way his name sounded. "If I promise to marry you, Akiva, will you promise to go to a house of study?"

He looked into her eyes for the first time. "Yes," he answered, and she could hear excitement in his voice. At that moment, she knew she had chosen the right man. And they promised to keep their plan a secret.

That night, Rachel's father came to her room. "One of the shepherds saw you sitting with Akiva. I must forbid you to see him again."

"Father," she answered, "I love you very much. But I love Akiva, too. In truth, I want to marry him."

Her father was angry. "That cannot be," he said fiercely. "I will find a rich man for you to marry."

"My heart is set on Akiva," Rachel answered.

"Then leave my house!" Kalba Savua yelled at her. "You shall not have even a single coin from me as long as you live."

So Rachel left her father's home and married Akiva. By the time winter set in, they were so poor they had to sleep in the straw bin where the donkeys fed. Akiva picked bits of straw from her hair and said, "If I were rich, I would give you a golden tiara such as the ladies of Jerusalem wear."

"I do not wish you were rich," she replied. "I wish what you wish: that you could read and write. Now, go to study Torah, as you promised me you would."

The next morning, Akiva left home. Rachel found work in town. After a time, she received a letter from Akiva. "How wonderful!" she thought. "Akiva has learned to read and write." In time, his letters became more beautiful. "How wonderful!" she thought. "He has learned so much." In this way, twelve years passed.

One day, she heard a commotion outside her door. She went out to see what was happening. A great teacher was entering the town, and hundreds of his students were following him. The people of the town came out to greet the teacher, and Rachel joined them. All at once, she recognized the teacher—it was her own Akiva at the head of all the students. She ran toward him, but the students tried to push her aside.

"Let her be," said Akiva to the students. "Everything that you and I know is only because of her." So saying, he hugged and kissed her.

Not a moment later, Kalba Savua pressed to the front of the crowd. When he saw Rachel and Akiva, he began to cry.

"Why are you crying?" asked Akiva gently.

"I made a vow that Rachel would never have even a single coin from me as long as she lived."

"Would you have made that vow if you had known that her husband would become a great teacher?" asked Akiva.

"If her husband had been able to read even a single word, I would never have made such a vow," answered Kalba Savua.

"I am her husband. I am the same Akiva who worked for you as a shepherd."

Then Kalba Savua looked at both Rachel and Akiva. "Forgive me, my children." And turning to Rachel, he added, "You and your husband shall have half of everything I have."

Forever after, Rabbi Akiva would say, "Rachel made me happy, wealthy, and wise: happy through her love for me; wealthy because she trusted me; and wise because she sent me to study Torah." (2,I:145)

From the Aggadah
THE SPICE OF SHABBAT

Rabbi Judah the Prince invited the emperor Antoninus to dine at his home on Shabbat. Because it was Shabbat, there was no fire for cooking, and the rabbi served the emperor cold dishes—salads and cheeses and cakes. The emperor ate and thanked Rabbi Judah for the wonderful meal.

Another time, on a weekday, Rabbi Judah asked Antoninus to come to dinner. This time, he served the emperor hot dishes.

The emperor thanked Rabbi Judah. Then he said, "It is strange, my friend. I liked the hot meal you served me tonight, but, in truth, I liked

the cold meal you served me on my last visit even more."

Rabbi Judah agreed, "These hot dishes are just fine, but they lack a secret spice."

Antoninus asked, "What spice would make a meal as delicious as the cold one? Tell me, and I will have my cooks send it to you."

"I do not think your cooks can send me this special spice," replied Rabbi Judah, laughing. "The secret spice is Shabbat." (2,I:325)

ONLY SIX DAYS

Rabbi Yohanan was walking with Rabbi Hiyya from Tiberius to Sepphoris. They came to a farm. "You see this farm," he said to Rabbi Hiyya. "I used to own this farm. I sold it so I could spend my time studying the Torah."

Walking a little farther, they came to a grove of olive trees. "You see these olive trees," Yohanan said. "I used to own them. I sold them so I could spend my time studying Torah."

Reaching the hills, they saw a vineyard with grapes hanging from every vine. "You see this vineyard," said Yohanan. "I used to own it. I sold it so I could spend my time studying Torah."

Suddenly, Rabbi Hiyya became very sad.

"Hiyya, my friend, what makes you so sad?" asked Yohanan.

"Looking at all you owned and all you sold makes me sad," replied Hiyya. "If you had kept these things, you would have been rich in your old age."

Rabbi Yohanan smiled. "Do you really think I was foolish? I sold things that were worth only six days, and I gained something that was worth forty days and forty nights. It took God only six days to create the entire world, but God spent forty days and forty nights revealing the Torah to Moses at Sinai." (2,I:406)

§ 8 ¿

Akiva Moves Mountains

Akiva was forty years old when he began to study Torah. He could neither read nor write. One day, standing by a hill, he saw water springing forth from a rock above him. He asked his friend, "Who opened up this stone to let the water out?"

His friend laughed. "Akiva, don't you know that water wears away stone?"

Akiva thought, "If soft water can break hard stone, then the words of Torah can break through my hard head."

How did he begin? He sat in a class with children. He took hold of one end of a writing tablet, and a child took hold of the other. The teacher wrote down *alef* and *bet* for Akiva, and he learned them. The teacher wrote the whole alphabet for him, and he learned it. The teacher wrote down a book of Torah for him, and he learned it. He studied until he learned the whole Torah.

Then he went where the older students sat with the great teachers Rabbi Eliezer and Rabbi Joshua. They explained a law to him, and he learned the law. Why was this law made? What good did this law do? When he knew the law well, he returned to his teachers and said,

"Teach me another law." He did this for twelve years until the teachers had no more to teach him.

One day, Akiva explained a law to Rabbi Eliezer. Rabbi Joshua said, "We have trained this student well although we hardly paid him any attention. Now he will be a greater teacher than either of us."

Rabbi Eliezer was puzzled. How had Akiva gained so much wisdom in such a short time?

Rabbi Simeon explained with a story. He said that Rabbi Akiva was like a stonecutter hacking away at a mountain. First, Akiva climbed to the top of the mountain and sat down. (That was like learning to read a single letter.) Then he took out his pick and began to chip small stones from the mountain. (That was like learning the alphabet.)

Then some fellows happened by and asked Akiva, "What are you doing?"

"I am going to hack away at this mountain until I move it all," Akiva replied.

The fellows were amazed. "Can you do such a thing?"

"Yes," said Akiva.

Akiva chipped away at the small stones until he came to a big boulder. (That was like learning a single law.) Then he took a piece of iron and wedged it under the boulder. He pried the boulder loose and sent it rolling off the mountain. (That was when he explained the law to Rabbi Eliezer.) Soon Akiva came to an even bigger boulder. He looked at the boulder and spoke to it, saying, "Your place is not here but there." Then he used his piece of iron to move even that boulder. (That was like using the teachings of Rabbi Eliezer and Rabbi Joshua to explain more laws.)

Rabbi Simeon said, "Akiva studied Torah the way a stonecutter cuts away a mountain. It is written in the Book of Job: 'He goes to

work upon the flinty rocks, he turns up mountains by the roots, he carves out channels through rock, and his eye sees every precious thing.' This tells how Akiva ben Joseph went from being our student to becoming our teacher." (2,I:146)

From the Aggadah
PRAISE AND WISDOM

The people of Simona sent word to Rabbi Judah the Prince, "Send us one of your rabbis who can be a teacher of Torah, a judge, a scribe, and a teacher for our children." Rabbi Judah sent Levi ben Sisi.

Levi went north to the town of Simona. When he arrived, the people made a great party for him. They gave him a beautiful house in which to live. They took him to the bathhouse and gave him new clothing. They brought him to the house of study and said, "We have made a throne for you to sit upon."

He climbed onto the platform they had built and sat on the throne of wood and silver. He placed his hands on the arms of the throne and looked down on the people of the town. "I am ready to help," he said.

Then they asked him a question about Jewish law. He could not answer. They asked him a question about Jewish legends. Again he could not answer. They asked him question after question, but he knew no answers whatever. At last, they told him, "You are not the kind of man we need." Levi left Simona and returned to Jerusalem.

The elders of Simona came to Rabbi Judah. "Is this the kind of man you send to us?" they asked. "He knows nothing of Jewish law and nothing of Jewish legend."

Judah sent for Levi and said to the elders of Simona, "Ask your questions again."

They asked the same questions. This time Levi gave an answer to each question. And in every answer there was the wisdom of Torah.

Rabbi Judah asked Levi, "Why are you able to answer these questions now when you could not answer them in Simona?"

"When I came to Simona," replied Levi, "they sat me on a throne and worshiped me like a god. My heart was full of pride, and all I could think was, 'How wonderful I must be to sit on a throne.' For the life of me, I could not remember any of the Torah that I had studied."

Rabbi Judah said, "They paid you honor because you studied Torah. But you forgot what Torah teaches: We must seek wisdom, not honor." (2,I:303)

PRAYING EVERY HOUR

The emperor Antoninus asked Rabbi Judah, "If the Jews are so close to God, why don't they pray to God every hour of the day?"

Rabbi Judah answered, "It is forbidden. If we prayed every hour of every day, we would soon grow tired of God, and God would soon grow tired of us."

"I think you are mistaken," said Antoninus.

What did Rabbi Judah do? Early the next morning, he went to Antoninus and said, "Hail to you, Emperor!" An hour later, he returned to Antoninus and said, "Hail to you, mighty Antoninus!" After another hour, he returned and said, "Peace be with you, great Caesar!"

After several hours of this, Antoninus grew angry. "Why do you treat me this way?" he asked Rabbi Judah.

Rabbi Judah replied, "I only wish to show you the truth of what I have said. If you, a man of flesh and blood, feel angered when I come every hour just to say hello, imagine how disturbed God would be if every Jew everywhere on earth prayed every hour of every day." (2,I:323)

❦ 9 ❦

Beruriah

Rabbi Meir married wise Beruriah, the daughter of Rabbi Hananiah. Other rabbis, friends of Meir, often spoke with Beruriah, finding that she knew the Torah and had studied the laws of Israel. When Meir and his friends were at the house of study, they would recall what Beruriah had said about this law or that verse, and they would agree, "Rightly did Beruriah say." Yet, it was not just what Beruriah said but what she did that spread her fame throughout Israel.

Beruriah and Rabbi Meir had two sons whom they loved very dearly. As the boys grew, they became students of Torah like their parents. Rabbi Meir took the boys to the synagogue every day. And in the house of study, they were the best pupils. Their parents were very proud of the boys.

Then a sickness passed through Jerusalem, taking many lives. Both boys came down with the illness on a Wednesday, and by Friday, they were hot with fever. All night, Meir and Beruriah sat with the boys, pressing cloths of cold water to their foreheads and praying for them to recover. In the morning, the boys fell into a deep sleep.

"The time has come for me to go to the synagogue," said Rabbi Meir.

Beruriah looked at the two sleeping children. "It will be all right," she said to her husband. "I will look after the boys." And Meir left home to pray the Sabbath morning service.

Rabbi Meir stayed at the synagogue nearly the whole day. After the morning prayers, he went into the house of study and taught. He spoke about the weekly Torah portion, explaining it and telling stories about it. But his thoughts were ever on his children. He kept watching for them to appear as they usually did. This Shabbat, however, the boys did not appear.

At home, Beruriah could do nothing to save the children. Though she watched over them and bathed them, their fever grew worse. They never awoke at all. Both of them died that afternoon. She covered them with a sheet, wiped the tears from her eyes, and prayed that God would be kind to them. Then she went into the kitchen and made a meal for Rabbi Meir.

As usual, Rabbi Meir came home from the synagogue in the late afternoon.

"Where are our sons?" he asked Beruriah.

"They went to the house of study," she said.

"I looked for them there but did not see them," said Rabbi Meir.

Beruriah did not reply. She handed Meir a cup of wine and said, "It is time for *Havdalah*. Let us not speak anymore until the peace of the Sabbath has departed."

So Rabbi Meir made the blessings of *Havdalah*, separating the Sabbath from the rest of the week. Then again he asked, "Where are our sons?"

"They went to play with their friends," said Beruriah, and she set the meal on the table. "They will be back soon."

Beruriah and Rabbi Meir finished the meal. Then Beruriah said, "My teacher, I have a question."

Meir nodded. "Ask your question."

"A while ago, a man came and gave me something to keep for him. Now he has returned to take back what he left. Shall I return it to him or not?"

Meir answered, "My love, you know the answer to this question. Of course, you must return a thing that has been given to you to hold for a time."

Beruriah said, "I needed to hear you say that so I would know it was the right thing to do." Then she took Meir by the hand and led him up to the bedroom. She pulled down the sheet, and Rabbi Meir saw that both children were dead.

Meir began to weep and cry, "My sons, my sons, my teachers, my teachers; my sons in the way of the world, but my teachers because through them I saw the Torah with new eyes."

Then Beruriah nodded. "Rabbi Meir, my husband, did you not say that I had to return a thing to its owner when the owner demanded it? Today God called for the two precious things that were given to us for a time, and I was forced to give them back."

"Why did you not tell me at once?" asked Meir, wiping his tears.

"On any other day of the week," Beruriah replied, "I would have told you at once. But today was the Sabbath, a day of peace, of rest, and of joy. Now that the Sabbath has gone, there is time enough for sadness." (2,I:205)

From the Aggadah
THE FOX AND THE TORAH

There came a time when the Romans declared that the teaching of Torah was forbidden throughout the Land of Israel. Pappus ben Judah found Rabbi Akiva teaching Torah in the marketplace. Pappus asked,

"Akiva, are you not afraid that the Romans will discover what you are doing and punish you?"

Rabbi Akiva replied, "I am doing what must be done. I can explain by telling you a parable about a fox and fishes." And Rabbi Akiva told this story:

ॐ A fox was once walking by the side of a river, and he saw fishes swimming back and forth in the stream. He called out to the fishes, "Why are you swimming back and forth as if you were fleeing from someone?"

They replied, "We are truly fleeing for our lives. We are afraid of the nets and the traps that people set to catch us."

Because the fox was hungry, he devised a plan. He said to the fishes, "How would you like me to take you out of the water so you will be safe from the traps and the nets?"

The fishes replied, "How foolish do you think we are? We are fearful today in the stream, where we can stay alive. How much more fearful would we be on the land, where we would surely die!"

"It is this way with us," said Rabbi Akiva. "If we are fearful when we sit and study the Torah, which is the life of the Jews, how much more fearful would we be if we were to stop studying the Torah. That would truly be the end of the Jews." (2,I:177)

RABBI MEIR AND THE BULLIES

Every day, on his way to the synagogue and on his way home, Rabbi Meir was bothered by a gang of bullies. "Ho, old man," they would say, "stand still and fight with us." Because Rabbi Meir hated fighting, he ran from the bullies.

One evening, he came home and told his wife, Beruriah, how the bullies had bothered him again. "I have prayed for these bullies to die," he said.

Beruriah was surprised. "Why did you pray for them to die?" she asked. "Do you not remember reading in the Torah, 'Let the wicked be no more'? Surely, the Torah means that when the bullies stop sinning against you, they will stop being wicked."

"What then should I have prayed?" Rabbi Meir inquired.

"You should have prayed that the bullies stop being bullies," Beruriah answered.

"You are truly wise, my wife," said Rabbi Meir, giving Beruriah a kiss. "That shall be my prayer from now on." (2,I:206)

§ 10 §

The Cave and the World

As they walked along a Roman road, Rabbi Judah said to Rabbi Simeon, "The Romans are a grand nation. Throughout our land, they pave the streets, construct bridges, and build baths."

Rabbi Simeon said, "No, the Romans are a selfish people. Whatever they make, they make for themselves. They pave roads so their armies can pass more easily. They construct bridges just to collect tolls from even the poorest people. And they build baths just to pamper themselves."

A man nearby overheard the words of Rabbi Simeon and repeated them to others. Soon the Roman emperor himself heard Rabbi Simeon's words. "No one should speak this way about mighty Rome. I shall have this man put to death for what he said," the emperor decreed. "Send the soldiers to seize him."

Rabbi Simeon heard that the Romans were coming to arrest him. He thought, "If I hide alone, the Romans will torture my wife and child until they tell where I am hidden. I will take my son and hide with him to keep him safe. And to keep my wife safe, I will not let her know where I am hidden."

So Rabbi Simeon and his son found a cave in the hills and hid in it.

The entrance to the cave was covered by thorns and vines. Yet from the small entrance, the cave opened up to a huge open space. Miraculously, Simeon and his son found a small spring of water in the cave and, beside it, a carob tree full of fruit. It was all they needed for food and drink. All day long, they studied the Torah. When it was time for prayer, each put on a *talit* and prayed. They took care of their robes, wearing them as little as possible so they would not fray. In this way, they passed twelve years in the cave.

In those days, there was a custom in Rome: When a Roman emperor died, all decrees of death against his enemies were forgiven. At the end of twelve years, the Roman emperor died. Now it was safe for Rabbi Simeon and his son to come out of hiding. But where were they hiding? No one knew. His friends did not know. His wife did not know. How could they be found?

A stranger came to Rabbi Simeon's wife. "I have a plan for finding your husband and your son," he said. "I have decided they must be hiding in a cave somewhere in the hills of Judea. I will go through the hills calling out to them until I am heard. Do not worry, I will find them for you."

Then the stranger went from hilltop to hilltop, crying out at every stop, "Who will tell Rabbi Simeon the emperor is dead and his decree has been set aside?"

Rabbi Simeon's wife was puzzled. "Who could this stranger be?" she asked Rabbi Judah.

Judah said, "Do not be afraid. This can be none other than the wandering Jew—the prophet Elijah—who goes from place to place, giving help wherever it is needed."

Inside the cave, Rabbi Simeon's son heard the words echoing from a hilltop, "Who will tell Rabbi Simeon the emperor is dead?" He ran to

his father. "Wonderful news, my father," he cried. "The emperor is dead. We can leave the cave and return home."

They put their robes over their loin cloths and made ready to leave the cave. As they cut through the vines at the cave's entrance, they were blinded by the bright sun. They stood still until they could see and then started for home. For the first time in twelve years, they saw some farmers plowing the fields.

"What are they doing?" asked Rabbi Simeon. "Why do they waste their time plowing the earth when they could be studying Torah. I shall teach them a lesson they will not soon forget." He raised his eyes to the heavens and pointed to the fields. With that, lightning struck where his finger pointed, and the fields burned as the farmers ran to safety.

They walked a little more, and they saw men gathering olives from a grove of olive trees.

"What are they doing?" asked Rabbi Simeon. "Why are they not studying Torah?" He pointed to the olive trees, and lightning struck them, setting the trees ablaze, sending the men scurrying off in all directions.

Suddenly, the stranger whose words had called them from their cave stood before them. "What are you doing, Rabbi Simeon?" he inquired. "God has sent me to ask you, 'Have you come out to destroy My world?' God says, 'Return to your cave and study the Torah again until you understand its words!'"

Then Rabbi Simeon and his son returned to the cave and studied the Torah for another twelve months. At the end of the twelve months, they heard a voice calling to them, saying, "Leave your cave. Let us see if you have learned to love both Torah and the world."

Rabbi Simeon and his son left the cave. This time, when they saw men picking olives from the olive trees, Rabbi Simeon said, "Blessed are those who make oil for the lamps of the house of study." And when they saw farmers in the fields, Rabbi Simeon said, "Blessed are those who help God to feed the hungry." (2,I:221)

From the Aggadah
THE CITY GUARDS

Resh Lakish taught: Rabbi Judah the Prince sent Rabbi Hiyya, Rabbi Ammi, and Rabbi Assi to all the small cities of the Land of Israel. In each city, they set up schools and found teachers for the children. Rabbi Judah taught: This is important work because the whole world

depends on the breath of schoolchildren. It is more important for children to study than for the Temple to be rebuilt.

Resh Lakish taught: When the rabbis came to a place where they found no teachers, they would say, "Bring us your city guards." When the people brought the soldiers who stood by the city gates, the rabbis would say, "You have brought us men of war. In the end, they may even destroy the city. Now bring us the city guards."

The people would be confused. "Who then are the real city guards?"

The rabbis answered, "The teachers of Torah, for they teach the love of God. As it is written in the Bible, 'If God does not guard the city, it is useless for the watchmen to stay awake.'" (2,I:449)

ONE LITTLE TOOTHPICK

Rabbi Ze'era was so old and weak that he needed help when he walked. Rabbi Haggai would walk with him, allowing Rabbi Ze'era to lean upon his shoulder. As they were walking one day, a man carrying a bundle of wood chips passed by them. Rabbi Ze'era said, "Good Rabbi Haggai, kindly stop that man and ask him for a single chip of wood that I may use as a toothpick."

Rabbi Haggai started after the man, but then he heard Rabbi Ze'era call him back. "Do not take even a single chip," Ze'era said. "I have thought about it, and I was wrong to ask this."

"Surely it cannot hurt to take a single chip from a whole bundle of wood chips," said Rabbi Haggai.

"Oh, it can hurt very much," Rabbi Ze'era responded. "If everyone would ask for but one chip, soon the man would have no bundle at all. God forbid that I should do such harm to this man." (2,I:509)

∮ 11 ∮

The Loving Couple

The wedding was the finest feast ever held in Sidon. It seemed that everyone had been invited. The bride was dressed in fine wool. They poured perfumed oil on her head and decorated her hair with a crown of gold. They bent the branch of an olive tree into a crown for her groom. And they set flowers all around the bridal canopy. The plates were large shells taken from the seashore, and there was wine and fish for everyone. The groom—a wealthy fisherman—was like a king, and his bride was like a queen. And all the Jews of Sidon praised the beauty of the bride and danced to celebrate the marriage.

One year passed and then another, but the fisherman and his wife were still without a child. Then the years went by more quickly until ten full years had passed.

One day, the woman said to her husband, "It seems that we shall never have a child together. You must leave me and marry another."

"I do not wish to leave you," answered the fisherman. "I love you very much."

"And I love you, too," said the woman, taking hold of his hand, "but to have a family you must have children, and we have no children."

The fisherman was sad. He hardly slept the whole night. In the morning, he told his wife, "I have heard that in Israel there is a great rabbi named Simeon ben Yohai. Perhaps he will bless us that we may have children."

The next day, they set out to the south to find the home of Rabbi Simeon ben Yohai. The fisherman and his wife held hands and from time to time, they glanced at each other with love. So it was for the three days of the journey, and they hardly spoke a word along the way. At last, they came to Rabbi Simeon.

"Great master of Torah," the fisherman said, "either you must bless us that we can have children or else we must part one from the other."

Rabbi Simeon shook his head. "This thing you ask is too difficult. The Torah tells us it takes three to make a child—a father, a mother, and God. It is clear that you wish to be a father. It is clear that your wife wishes to be a mother. But God alone decides when the time is right."

"Does this mean we must be divorced?" asked the fisherman's wife.

"Yes," said Rabbi Simeon, seeing their bodies bending in pain and their faces growing long. "But I declare you must separate in joy and not in sadness. You have told me how wonderful was the feast at your wedding. Now, you must make a feast just as wonderful for your divorce. You shall be separated with food, with wine, and with love."

They left the rabbi and returned to Sidon. Along the way, when the wife would begin to cry, her husband would say, "Why should you cry? Think of the beautiful feast we shall soon have." And when the husband would start to weep, his wife would say, "This is no time for weeping. We must think about who should be invited to our feast."

Then they made a great feast, setting out the seashell plates, cooking fish and roasting lamb, making bread and baking cakes, and bring-

ing wine in great jugs to the tables. It seemed that all the Jews of Sidon were invited, and the dancing, singing, and drinking went on from evening to the early hours of the next morning. Even as the last cup of wine was passed, and the last dance was danced, the fisherman and his wife were filled with the joy of celebration.

Then the fisherman said to his wife, "My love, you may choose anything precious from my home and bring it with you when you return to your father's house."

What did she do? After the fisherman fell asleep, she called her servants and told them, "Lift the couch with my husband on it, and carry the couch and my husband to my father's house."

That night, the fisherman rose from his sleep and looked around. "My love, where am I?" he asked.

"Do you not know?" she asked. "You are in the house of my father."

"But what am I doing in the house of your father?"

"Do you not know? You said to me last night: 'Choose anything precious from my home and bring it with you when you return to your father's house.' There is nothing in the world more precious to me than you."

The fisherman took his wife in his arms. "I shall never leave you," he said. "We shall return to Rabbi Simeon, and this time he will pray with us."

And when they came to Rabbi Simeon, he said, "I am pleased that you have returned and even more pleased that you have learned a lesson. The last time, you asked me to pray for you. That is fine, but not enough. This time, you ask me to pray with you. So let us pray together, for it is when we pray together that God hears us best."

A season passed before the fisherman's wife took her husband's hand, saying, "My love, place your hand just here and feel the life that is growing. Together—God and you and I—we shall soon have a child." (2,I:224)

From the Aggadah
THE VALLEY OF GOLD

A student of Rabbi Simeon ben Yohai went to sea. When the student returned, he brought with him a chest of gold. Rabbi Simeon asked, "How did you become so rich?"

The student said, "I traded this for that, a small thing for a thing slightly larger, then a larger thing for a thing even larger. In the end, I had traded so many times that I had a chest filled with golden coins."

"It is good," Rabbi Simeon said. But he was soon to change his mind.

When the other students saw the riches, they grew jealous. They came to Rabbi Simeon and said, "Let us all go to sea so all of us might return with gold."

Rabbi Simeon said, "Forget this idea. Come along with me to the house of study." But the students no longer wished to study Torah. Rabbi Simeon would say, "The law teaches us this," and the students would say, "When can we go down to the sea?"

At last, Rabbi Simeon said, "You do not need to leave the Land of Israel to become wealthy. I will take you to where there is more gold than anyone can carry."

They followed him to a valley near Mount Meron. They watched as the rabbi began to pray. They heard him say, "Valley, O valley, fill up with coins of gold." Then the olives disappeared from the olive trees, and gold coins hung where every olive had been. The water in the streams stopped flowing, and the riverbeds were filled with gold coins

instead of pebbles. Gold coins rolled down from the top of Mount Meron until the floor of the valley was paved with gold from one end to the other. Gold coins gathered in small heaps around the sandals of the students. Gold glittered at the tops of every bush.

"Is it gold you want?" asked Rabbi Simeon. "Here is more gold than anyone can carry. You can take as much of it as you wish."

The students yelled with joy. Laughing and singing, they gathered gold until they could carry no more. When they had enough, they came back to the rabbi to thank him.

The rabbi told them: "You may not wish to thank me for this. Look around. You have gathered as many gold coins as you can carry, and there is still gold everywhere."

The students looked, and it was so.

Then Rabbi Simeon said: "It is the same with Torah. You can take as much of the riches of Torah as you can carry, and there will always be more Torah than any one person can take. Yet there is a difference between the gold coins and the Torah. When you have finished spending the coins, you will have nothing left. When you die, you will not take gold coins with you to the next world. But with Torah, you can teach all you want, and you will still have all you have learned. And when you die, you will be able to take your learning with you to the next world. It is up to you to choose. Which would you rather have, Torah or gold?"

Then every student dropped the gold coins. Water returned to the stream. Olives returned to the branches of the olive trees. And the floor of the valley was green with grass and dotted with flowers. And Rabbi Simeon smiled at his students, saying, "You have chosen wisely." (2,I:223)

WHAT IS MOST PRECIOUS?

Ardavan, the king of Parthia, sent a costly pearl to Rav with a message, saying, "Send me something equally precious in return for this pearl." In return, Rav sent a *mezuzah* to Ardavan.

Ardavan sent back a message to Rav, saying, "I sent you something so valuable that it could not be bought by anyone but a king, and you have sent me something that every Jew has, and anyone can buy."

This time, Rav wrote a message for the king: "O king of Parthia, what I have sent you is worth much more than what you sent me. You have sent me a pearl that I must guard day and night; I sent you a *mezuzah* that will guard *you* at your going out and at your coming in." (2,I:542)

§ 12 §

The Messiah

Rabbi Joshua ben Levi was visiting the grave of Rabbi Simeon ben Yohai. As he stood by the entrance to the cave where Simeon was buried, a stranger suddenly appeared beside him. "From where did you come?" Rabbi Joshua inquired.

The stranger shrugged. "I have wandered here and wandered there."

"There is only one who would give this answer," Rabbi Joshua said. "You must be the prophet Elijah, who wanders through the world waiting for the time when the Messiah will come."

The stranger shrugged a second time. "You have decided," he said. "And you must be Rabbi Joshua ben Levi."

"You are Elijah!" said Rabbi Joshua. "What other stranger would know my name? By your life, tell me when the Messiah will come."

The stranger smiled and said, "Go and ask him yourself."

"Where shall I find him?" Rabbi Joshua asked.

"He is sitting with the beggars at the entrance to the city of Rome."

"And how shall I know him?" asked Rabbi Joshua.

"He is easy to find," said the stranger. "Like the other beggars, his body is covered with sores and wrapped with bandages. The other beggars unwrap all their bandages to let the sun and air heal their sores. But the Messiah unwraps only one bandage at a time. In this way, when God calls for the Messiah to appear, he will have only one bandage to wrap, and so he will not be delayed. You see, Rabbi Joshua, the Messiah is easy to find."

Rabbi Joshua set forth on the long journey to Rome. He traveled on foot to the sea and by ship across the sea. When he came to the gate of the city, he saw the Messiah, the only beggar with only one bandage untied. As he came close, he raised one hand to greet the Messiah. "Peace be with you, Joshua ben Levi," the Messiah returned.

"The Jews have suffered much," said Rabbi Joshua. "Our Temple has been destroyed by Rome, and our heroes have been defeated. The Romans do not allow us to study the Torah in peace. We long for an end to our suffering."

"I know the suffering of the Jewish people," said the Messiah. "Every sore on my body is a sign of your troubles. And every sore on the bodies of the other beggars is a sign of the troubles of all the other peoples of God's world. Even the Romans suffer. Yet God is ready to put an end to the troubles of the world."

Rabbi Joshua wanted an answer he could understand. "O master, tell me when you will come to put an end to our suffering."

The Messiah answered, "Today."

Rabbi Joshua did not tarry. He went down to the sea and traveled by ship to the Land of Israel. A storm came up, and waves tossed the ship from side to side. The day came and went, and so did the next, and the storm blew fiercely. Even the sailors were ill, and Rabbi Joshua saw that suffering continued all around him. When, at last, he reached Israel, he made his way by foot to the cave where Rabbi

Simeon was buried. Many days had passed, and still the Messiah had not appeared.

The stranger was waiting for Rabbi Joshua by the cave. "Did the Messiah give you an answer?" the stranger asked.

"The Messiah said, 'Peace be with you, Joshua ben Levi.'"

The stranger nodded. "This means that you and your family will have peace in the time of the Messiah."

Rabbi Joshua shrugged. "How can I believe this is true when the Messiah also lied to me?"

"What did the Messiah say that you did not believe?" the stranger demanded.

"I asked him when he would come to put an end to the suffering of the world, and the Messiah told me today. Yet he did not come that day or any day since."

The stranger smiled. "The Messiah has spoken the truth. He has given you the beginning of a verse from the Bible. It is written there, 'Today—if you would only listen to God's voice.'"

"Please teach me what that means," said Rabbi Joshua.

"It means that the Messiah can come any day, even this very day, if only the people listen to the voice of God, who commanded us to live in peace."

"I still do not understand," Rabbi Joshua said. "If we bring peace to the world, we will have no need of the Messiah."

The stranger nodded. "You do understand," he replied. "As soon as we do not need the Messiah, the time of the Messiah will come. Teach peace and pursue peace, and the day of the Messiah can be today."
(2,I:394)

From the Aggadah
THE MEAL

A beggar came to the door of Rava, asking for a meal. The teacher asked him, "What do you usually eat?"

The beggar answered, "Bread and chicken, figs and dates, olives and pickles are my food. For drink, I take a fine wine. For dessert, I eat cakes covered in honey."

"It is very costly to feed you!" Rava remarked. "If you eat like that every night, the whole community can hardly afford to give you food."

The beggar shook his head. "I do not eat the food of the community. I eat the food God provides for everyone. Is it not true, my master, that God provides all food?"

Just then, Rava's sister came to the door. He had not seen her in many years. He greeted her and kissed her. Then he asked her what she was carrying. "I have brought you many fine things to eat," she said. "In my bag are dates and figs, pickles and olives, and a chicken fit for a king."

Rava turned to the beggar. "You are right," he laughed. "God does provide for us. Come in and share our meal." (2,I:710)

ONE AFTER ANOTHER

Our rabbis taught: When Rabbi Akiva died, Rabbi Judah the Prince was born. When Rabbi Judah the Prince died, Rabbi Yudan was born. When Rabbi Yudan died, Rava was born. When Rava died, Rabbi Ashi was born.

So we learn that a righteous person does not leave this world until another righteous person is brought into being.

One of the students asked, "When a righteous person dies, how do we know who the next righteous person will be?"

Our rabbis taught: It could be you. We never know until your life also comes to an end. For everything depends on the way you live your life. (2,I:793)

A Chronology of the Sages

The second part of *Sefer Ha-Aggadah*, "The Deeds of the Sages," is arranged chronologically. We have generally followed this pattern. From time to time, however, we rearranged the stories to bring a unity of theme or character to a particular chapter. The sages are listed below in the order of their appearance in this volume. The dates given are those assigned by Bialik and Ravnitzky.

- Simeon ben Shetah — fl. first century B.C.E.
- Honi the Circle Maker — fl. second half of the first century B.C.E.
- Hillel the Elder — fl. end of the first century B.C.E.
- Yohanan ben Zakkai — first century
- Hanina ben Dosa — fl. first century
- Joshua ben Hananiah — fl. ca. 90–130
- Eliezer ben Hyrcanus — fl. second century
- Tarfon — fl. ca. 110–135
- Akiva — fl. 95–135
- Yose ben Halafta — fl. second half of the second century
- Nahum the Man of Gamzo — fl. ca. 90–130

- Judah bar Ilai — second half of the second century
- Judah I, the Patriarch (Judah the Prince) — fl. last quarter of the second century to the beginning of the third century

- Hiyya the Elder — fl. last quarter of the second century to the beginning of the third century

- Meir (and Beruriah) — fl. ca. 130–160
- Simeon ben Yohai — fl. ca. 130–160
- Simeon ben Lakish (Resh Lakish) — second half of the second century
- Zera (Ze'era) — fl. first half of the fourth century
- Rav (Abba bar Aibu) — fl. 219–247
- Joshua ben Levi — fl. first half of the third century
- Rava bar Joseph bar Hama — fl. 299–352
- Judah II (Yudan the Patriarch) — fl. 225–253
- Ashi — 352–427

About the Author

SEYMOUR ROSSEL is the chief executive officer of Pathways Foundation; the president of Rossel Computer Consulting, Inc.; and author of twenty-six books for Jewish and public schools, including the two-volume best-seller *A Child's Bible; Journey through Jewish History; The Holocaust; Israel: Covenant People, Covenant Land;* and *A Thousand and One Chickens.*

§⸙

About the Illustrator

JUDY DICK, a graduate of Yeshiva University, attended the Fashion Institute of Technology and holds a degree in illustration from Pratt Institute. She is a freelance illustrator, who has coordinated art and Jewish studies, while working on projects in the United States, Israel, and the former Soviet Union.